SUPERCARS

TESLA

Helen Lepp Friesen

www.openlightbox.com

Step 1
Go to **www.openlightbox.com**

Step 2
Enter this unique code
FCUYILKPM

Step 3
Explore your interactive eBook!

AV2 is optimized for use on any device

Your interactive eBook comes with...

Contents
Browse a live contents page to easily navigate through resources

Audio
Listen to sections of the book read aloud

Videos
Watch informative video clips

Weblinks
Gain additional information for research

Slideshows
View images and captions

Try This!
Complete activities and hands-on experiments

Key Words
Study vocabulary, and complete a matching word activity

Quizzes
Test your knowledge

Share
Share titles within your Learning Management System (LMS) or Library Circulation System

Citation
Create bibliographical references following the Chicago Manual of Style

This title is part of our AV2 digital subscription

1-Year K–5 Subscription
ISBN 978-1-7911-3320-7

Access hundreds of AV2 titles with our digital subscription.
Sign up for a FREE trial at **www.openlightbox.com/trial**

SUPERCARS

TESLA

CONTENTS

TE

SLA

TESLA SUPERCARS

Car makers pay special attention to detail when building supercars. These cars are designed to be elegant and go fast. They have powerful engines and are made with luxurious materials. A limited number of supercars are made each year. This makes them exclusive.

Tesla is one of the most important car companies in the United States. It makes electric vehicles, including supercars. Founded in 2003, the company has quickly become the worldwide leader in electric vehicle sales.

The **most expensive Tesla** is a Model S with gold-plated parts. It costs **$299,999**.

Tesla delivered **499,550** cars to customers in **2020**.

EBERHARD, TARPENNING, AND MUSK

Martin Eberhard and Marc Tarpenning are both **engineers**. In 2003, they founded Tesla Motors, Inc. They wanted to make electric sports cars. In 2004, Elon Musk, a successful **entrepreneur**, became a major **investor** in Tesla. Tesla's first car, the Roadster, arrived on the market in 2008. That same year, Eberhard and Tarpenning left the company. Musk became **chief executive officer (CEO)** of Tesla. In the following years, he worked to launch new vehicles. He also helped Tesla expand into the energy storage systems market.

The Roadster was first revealed in Santa Monica, California, in 2006.

MAP OF THE UNITED STATES

Tesla's headquarters and main car factory are currently in California. Its electric batteries, solar panels, and energy storage systems are made in Nevada and New York.

World Map

Canada

Tesla Factory, Fremont, California

Gigafactory 1, Reno, Nevada

Tesla Headquarters, Palo Alto, California

Gigafactory 2, Buffalo, New York

Atlantic Ocean

Mexico

Pacific Ocean

N
W
E
S

SCALE 0 500 Kilometers 500 Miles

LEGEND

- Key Location
- United States
- Land
- Water

THE T LOGO

Tesla was named after Nikola Tesla, an inventor born in the 19th century. Nikola Tesla is best known for designing the **alternating current** system. Most Tesla vehicles use this system to run. Tesla asked a design firm called RO Studio to design its logo. The firm came up with a logo that looks like a T, for Tesla. However, the logo has a hidden meaning. Its shape represents parts of an electric motor.

RO Studio also designed the logo for SpaceX, the aerospace company founded by Elon Musk in 2002.

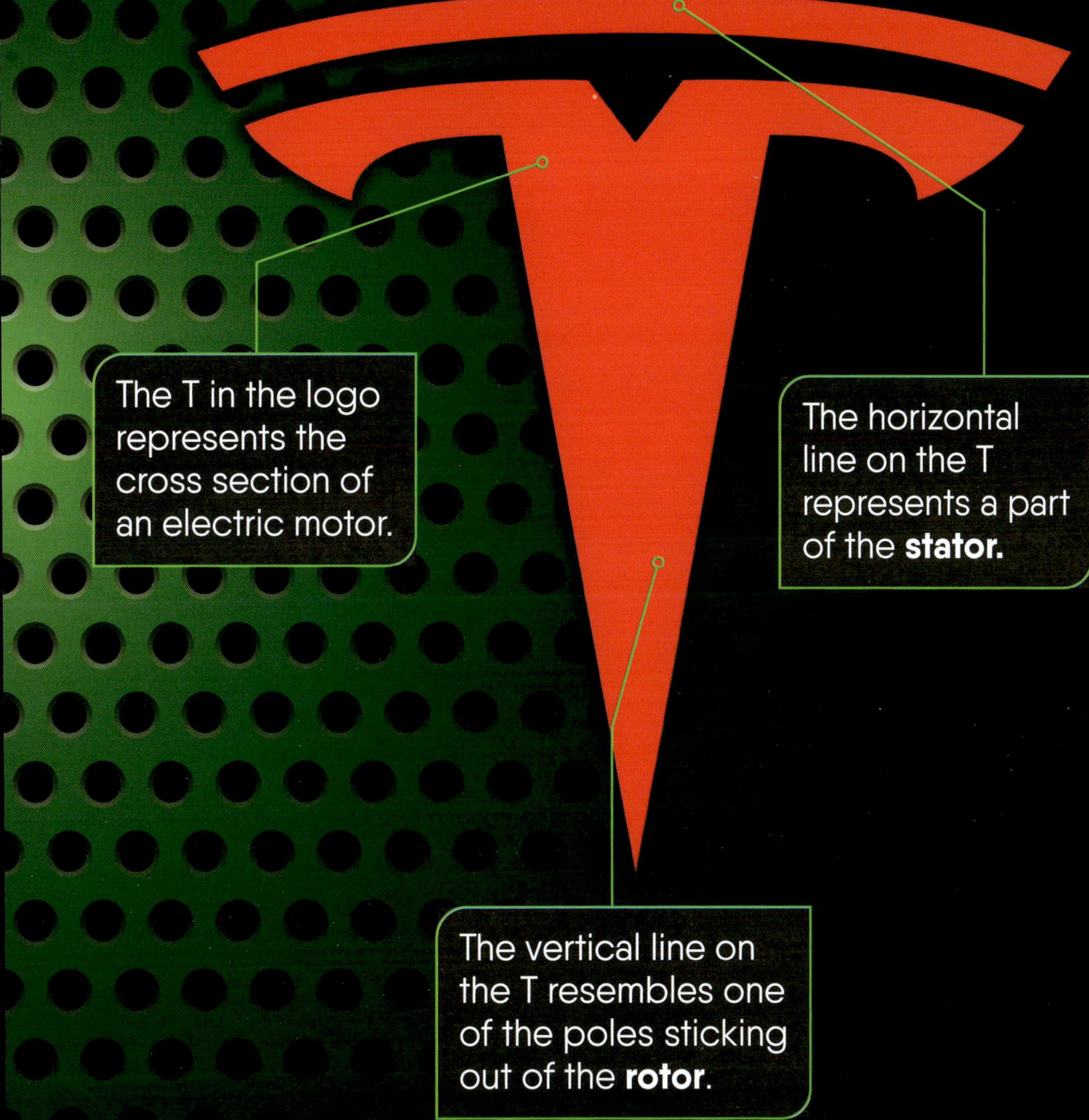
The T in the logo represents the cross section of an electric motor.
The horizontal line on the T represents a part of the **stator.**
The vertical line on the T resembles one of the poles sticking out of the **rotor**.

TESLA THROUGH HISTORY

Tesla's first goal was to make an all-electric sports car. Today, the company leads the world's electric vehicle market.

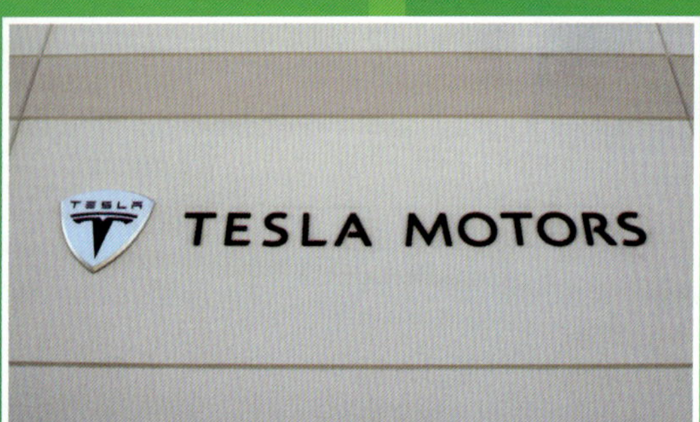

Tesla Motors, Inc. is founded in 2003. The company's name is changed to Tesla, Inc. in 2017.

2003

2004

Elon Musk invests in Tesla. He also becomes Tesla's **chairman of the board**.

2010

Tesla becomes a public company. It starts selling stock to investors to raise funds for new projects.

Tesla unveils the Powerwall system. It follows the Tesla Solar Roof that was revealed in 2015. Together, these systems allow a home to absorb energy from the Sun and store it for future use.

Construction on a new Tesla factory begins in Austin, Texas. The factory is expected to have more than 10,000 employees by 2022.

2016

2019

2020

The first Tesla Gigafactory outside the United States opens in Shanghai, China. Another Gigafactory is under construction in Berlin, Germany.

FAMOUS TESLAS

Even though Tesla was only founded in 2003, its models have already drawn attention from Hollywood. A Tesla Roadster can be seen in the garage of Tony Stark, the main character in the popular superhero film *Iron Man*. One of the characters in the animated movie *Cars 3*, Natalie Certain, is said to be inspired by the Tesla Model S.

Movies have also provided ideas for some Tesla vehicles. Elon Musk noted that the design for an upcoming Tesla model, the Cybertruck, was influenced by the Lotus Esprit. Musk first saw this car in the James Bond film *The Spy Who Loved Me*.

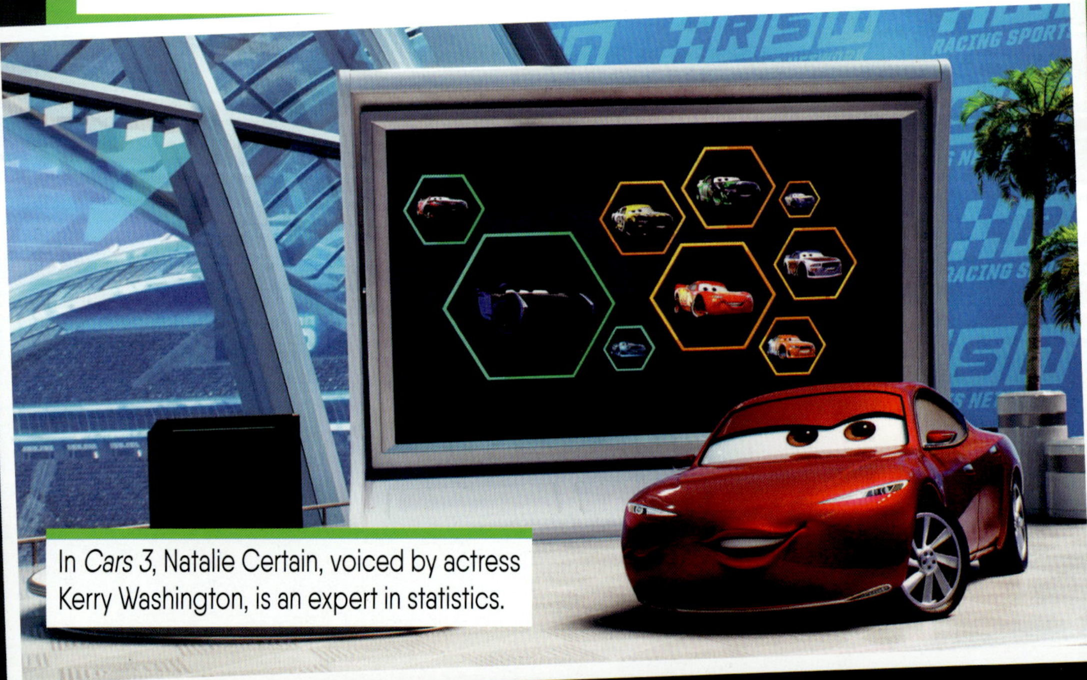

In *Cars 3*, Natalie Certain, voiced by actress Kerry Washington, is an expert in statistics.

Many celebrities have chosen to drive Tesla cars. Famed actor Leonardo DiCaprio strongly believes in protecting the environment. He is often seen driving electric cars, including a Tesla Roadster. Renowned director Steven Spielberg and actors Ben Affleck, Matt Damon, and Will Smith are other Tesla lovers in Hollywood.

Steven Spielberg drives a Tesla Model S.

Ben Affleck also drives a Model S.

In *The Spy Who Loved Me*, a Lotus Esprit could turn into a submarine. Elon Musk purchased the car used in the movie in 2013.

AT THE RACES

Tesla does not have an official racing team yet. In the United States, private drivers have used Tesla cars for autocross competitions. Teslas are also used for other types of races. In 2021, a race-modified Model S Plaid won the exhibition class of the Pikes Peak International Hill Climb race, in Colorado.

In 2018, the Fédération Internationale de l'Automobile (FIA), or International Automobile Federation, approved a new international racing championship called Electric Production Car Series (EPCS). EPCS is supposed to feature only Tesla Model S P100D cars specially modified for racing. However, the championship start date has not yet been announced.

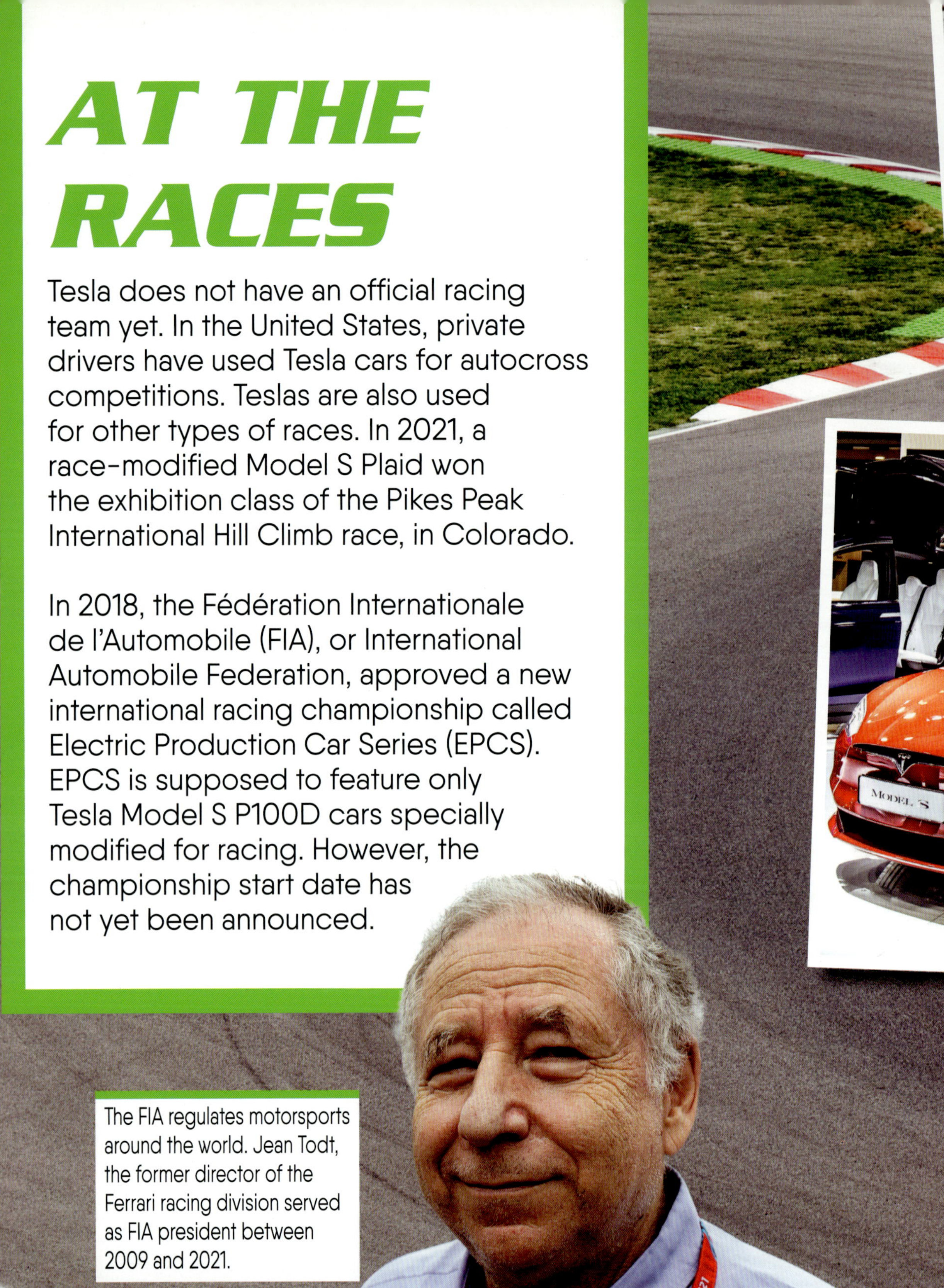

The FIA regulates motorsports around the world. Jean Todt, the former director of the Ferrari racing division served as FIA president between 2009 and 2021.

In autocross, traffic cones are used to create road courses. Drivers race to complete a course in the lowest time without hitting any cones.

To race in EPCS, Tesla Model S P100Ds will be modified to be about 1,100 pounds (500 kilograms) lighter and have higher horsepower.

The **FIA** was founded in **1904**.

EPCS plans to include **10 racing teams**, each with **2 drivers**.

Another important motorsport for electric cars recognized by FIA is Formula E, a championship for single-seater electric cars. Tesla does not plan to race in Formula E at the moment.

HOW IT'S MADE

Tesla's factory in Fremont, California, currently covers an area of almost 5.4 million square feet (500,000 square meters). The assembly lines in the Fremont factory use state-of-the-art robots and different assembly machines. Engineers at Tesla work to make the production process more efficient. They adjust the settings of robots and assembly machines to make them work faster and better. Tesla also relies on skilled craftspeople to complete the production process.

Elon Musk plans to increase Tesla's production to 20 million vehicles a year by 2030. The new Gigafactories in Shanghai, Berlin, and Austin will help him reach this target.

The Fremont plant produces all the Tesla models currently on the market.

As of 2020, Tesla has more than 70,700 employees worldwide.

Tesla earned **$31.5 billion** in **2020.**

It takes about **90 minutes** to build a **Model 3.**

Tesla purchased the Fremont factory in 2010.

The Gigafactory in Shanghai, China, can make up to 5,000 Model 3s a week.

TODAY'S LINEUP

Tesla started with sports cars. It now makes different types of vehicles. The Model S and Model 3 are sedans. The Model X and Model Y are sport utility vehicles (SUVs).

People can customize a Tesla to make it more suitable to their needs. Tesla's customers can also choose to add futuristic **autopilot** features to their vehicles.

Here are some of the Teslas on the road today.

Tesla Model Y Long Range

Engine: **Dual Motor All-Wheel Drive**

Range: **326 miles (525 km)**

0–60 mph (0–100 km/h): **4.8 seconds**

Starting Price: **$53,990**

Tesla Model X Long Range

Engine: **Dual Motor All-Wheel Drive**

Range: **360 miles (579 km)**

0–60 mph (0–100 km/h): **3.8 seconds**

Starting Price: **$94,990**

Tesla Model S Plaid

Engine: **Tri Motor All-Wheel Drive**

Range: **396 miles (637 km)**

0–60 mph (0–100 km/h): **1.9 seconds**

Starting Price: **$122,990**

TOMORROW'S TESLA

Since its foundation, Tesla has focused on reducing the environmental impact of cars. This remains Tesla's main objective for the future. The company plans to offer electric options to a larger audience by creating different types of vehicles. Tesla has already unveiled a new truck called the Cybertruck, along with a **semi** and an updated version of the Roadster. These vehicles are all due to arrive on the market in the coming years. The company is also developing new compact vehicles, as well as affordable cars.

The Tesla Semi is expected to have a range of about 621 miles (1,000 km).

Elon Musk plans to release a new $25,000 electric car by 2023.

The glass roof of the new Roadster can be removed and stored in the trunk.

The Cybertruck has a super-resistant external shell made of stainless steel.

TESLA QUIZ

1. Who voiced the Natalie Certain's character in *Cars 3*?

2. When did Elon Musk become Tesla's CEO?

3. What does the Tesla's T logo represent?

4. When was the FIA founded?

5. Where is Tesla's main car factory?

6. When was SpaceX founded?

7. Which car influenced the design of the Cybertruck?

8. When did Tesla become a public company?

9. How long does it take to build a Model 3?

10. How many cars did Tesla deliver in 2020?

ANSWERS

1 Kerry Washington **2** In 2008
3 The T in Tesla and the cross section of an electric motor
4 In 1904 **5** California **6** In 2002
7 The Lotus Esprit **8** In 2010
9 90 minutes **10** 499,550

KEY WORDS

alternating current: an electric current that reverses its direction many times per second at regular intervals

autopilot: a device that keeps vehicles moving without human control

chairman of the board: the person who leads a group of people that oversee the activity of a company

chief executive officer (CEO): the highest ranking manager in a company

engineers: people trained in how to build things and use different materials

entrepreneur: someone who comes up with an idea and starts a business based on that idea

investor: a person who puts money into a company, a property, or a financial plan with the expectation of generating profit

rotor: a moving part in an electric motor

semi: a large truck made of a vehicle that pulls a large container

stator: coils in an electric motor

INDEX

Get the best of both worlds.

AV2 bridges the gap between print and digital.

The expandable resources toolbar enables quick access to content including **videos**, **audio**, **activities**, **weblinks**, **slideshows**, **quizzes**, and **key words**.

Animated videos make static images come alive.

Resource icons on each page help readers to further **explore key concepts**.

Published by Lightbox Learning
276 5th Avenue, Suite 704 #917
New York, NY 10001
Website: www.openlightbox.com

Library of Congress Cataloging-in-Publication Data

Names: Friesen, Helen Lepp, 1961- author.
Title: Tesla / Helen Lepp Friesen.
Description: New York, NY : AV2, 2021. | Series: Supercars | Includes index. | Audience: Grades 2-3
Identifiers: LCCN 2021022187 (print) | LCCN 2021022188 (ebook) | ISBN 9781791138905 (library binding) | ISBN 9781791138912 (paperback) | ISBN 9781791138929 (ebook other)
Subjects: LCSH: Tesla automobiles--Juvenile literature. | Sports car racing--Juvenile literature.
Classification: LCC TL215.T43 F75 2021 (print) | LCC TL215.T43 (ebook) | DDC 629.222/2--dc23
LC record available at https://lccn.loc.gov/2021022187
LC ebook record available at https://lccn.loc.gov/2021022188

Printed in Guangzhou, China
1 2 3 4 5 6 7 8 9 0 25 24 23 22 21

072021
101120

Art Director: Terry Paulhus
Project Coordinator: Sara Cucini

Photo Credits
Every reasonable effort has been made to trace ownership and to obtain permission to reprint copyright material. The publisher would be pleased to have any errors or omissions brought to its attention so that they may be corrected in subsequent printings. The publisher acknowledges Getty Images, Alamy, Shutterstock, and Dreamstime as its primary image suppliers for this title.